GREAT
THINGS
ABOUT
BEING
Gay

·

501 GREAT THINGS ABOUT BEING *Gay*

•

E D W A R D   T A U S S I G

A Wonderland Press Book

Andrews McMeel Publishing

Kansas City

www.andrewsmcmeel.com

98 99 00 01 02•BAM•10 9 8 7 6 5 4 3 2 1

Library of Congress Cataloging-in-Publication Data

Taussig, Edward
501 great things about being gay/Edward Taussig.
p. cm.
ISBN 0-8362-5416-3 (pbk.)
1. Homosexuality—Humor. 2. Gay men—Humor.
3. Gay wit and humor. I. Title.
PN6231.H57T38 1998   97–49980
818.5402—dc21   CIP

Design by Tanya Maiboroda

ATTENTION: SCHOOLS AND BUSINESSES
Andrews McMeel books are available at quantity
discounts with bulk purchase for educational, busi-
ness, or sales promotional use. For information,
please write to: Special Sales Department, Andrews
McMeel Publishing, 4520 Main Street, Kansas City,
Missouri 64111.

Dedicated

to the memory of

Chris Eymard Doran (1953–1997).

Laughing with him was one of the

great things about being gay.

ACKNOWLEDGMENTS

The author wishes to thank John Campbell of The Wonderland Press for being both inspiration and laugh track. He also wishes to thank Yone Akiyama, Doug Bartow, Jeanie Bryson, Maura Dausey, Ellen Dennis, Missy and Carlos Falchi, Vicki and Alex Gershwin, Grey Advertising, Suzanne Klotz, Sam Penrod, and the author's parents, for being both appreciative and supportive. And Fernando, Francisco, Luciano, Norberto, Paulo, and especially Sergio for being, well...never mind. Oh, one more: Daniel Day–Lewis. Just for being.

501
GREAT
THINGS
ABOUT
BEING
Gay

You truly *don't* care
who Julia Roberts is
sleeping with.

•

You understand the subtle
differences between forty-
three brands of imported
"luxury" vodka.

•

We've got Cole Porter.
They've got Paul Anka.

You can call anyone
"honey." Including pets.

•

You know someone
who definitely was in
that emergency room
with Richard Gere
and the gerbil.

•

You understand the
immense importance
of good lighting.

3

You can be at a crowded disco the size of two football fields, and still spot a toupee.

＊

You can tell a woman you love her bathing suit, and mean her bathing suit.

4

You can tell a woman she's
got lipstick on her teeth
without embarrassing her.

◆

You never have to
spend an evening at a
karaoke bar.

You know how to get
your mother off the
phone quickly.

*

You can explain the
nuances between "steady
date," "boyfriend,"
and "lover."

*

You really have "been
there, done that."

Your women friends will tell you everything you want to know about their boyfriends. And that means everything.

•

No one expects you to kiss and *not* tell.

•

You're the only type of male who gets to say "fabulous."

You can have naked
pictures of men you don't
know in your home.

*

You can have naked
men you don't know in
your home.

You know someone who's slept with:

a. Tom Cruise
b. Tom Selleck
c. Rock Hudson
d. Gary Cooper
e. Rudolph Valentino
f. Ludwig of Bavaria

●

You've slept with _____. *(fill in the blank)*

You never have to learn
how to play golf.

•

You don't ever have to
listen to "a little fatherly
advice."

•

Unlike your women
friends, you can hang out
in men's locker rooms.

You can dress like a
member of a college
crew team without ever
having to break a sweat.

•

You know how to handle
the telephone like a
Stradivarius.

You understand why the good Lord invented spandex.

You understand why the good Lord didn't intend everyone to wear it.

You know the differences
between a latte, a
macchiato, a café au lait,
and a cappucino. And
if you don't, you know
how to fake it.

•

In the shower, you look
like:

a. Michelangelo's David
b. Michelangelo's Adam
c. Michelangelo's mother

You know how to get back
at just about everyone.

*

You never have to go to a
Rosanna Arquette movie.

*

Your pets always have
great names.

You don't have to sit
through cute baby stories.

•

Nobody expects you to
change the tire.

•

You're the only kind of
guy who gets to do the
Cosmo quizzes.

You never have to run out
for tampons.

*

You know how to get the
waiter's attention.

*

You only wear polyester
when you mean to.

At any given instant,
you can recite who was
gay since the dawn of
recorded history.

•

You are, hands down,
your nephews' and nieces'
favorite uncle.

•

You get to choose your
family.

17

You know the salient traits
of the zodiac. And if not,
you know how to look
interested as someone
belabors them.

※

You can tell your sexual
compatibility with a
potential partner by the
way he holds his drink.

You can smile to let someone know you can't stand them.

•

You do a great impression of:

a. Bette Davis
b. your mother
c. yourself

You wouldn't be caught
dead in Hooters.

❖

You can freeze a troll from
twenty feet away.

❖

You're good pals with
women other people
can't stand.

You've always got
an opinion.

●

You've read the book,
seen the movie, done
the musical.

●

You know how to
"air kiss."

You make a great cup
of coffee.

•

You know exactly which
cosmetic surgery to
consider having . . . and
which excuses you'll give
when people ask you
where you've been for
two weeks.

The only trend you're not way ahead of is cigar smoking.

You've got a novel theory to explain why it's popular, however.

You know how to dress
strategically.

•

You know when to
move out.

•

Your car has an amusing
female name.

You're the only one at the
reunion who looks a lot
better than you did in
high school.

•

You've got at least one
framed picture of a pet.

•

You're on a first-name
basis with at least one
cabaret performer.

If your mattress could
talk, it would be
Joan Rivers.

•

You know that sex
complicates things. So?

•

You'd never dream of
hiring a woman for her
cup size.

When you can't get
foie gras, you'll settle
for salami.

●

You know that being
called "a cheap slut" isn't
actually an insult.

There's a
married man
somewhere
who is terrified
of you.

You're someone's favorite candidate for the turkey baster.

●

You can insult straight guys' taste in ties.

●

You wouldn't buy someone a mug for his birthday.

You'll never have to
be a soccer mom.
You can, however,
be a diva.

✳

You're the only kind of
person over the age of
forty who still sports the
occasional hickey.

You never have to watch
a kiddie movie.

•

You understand a man's
physiology better than
Leonardo da Vinci.
(Well, better than Picasso
anyway...)

•

You've insulted a bigot.

31

Nobody tells
you what to do
in bed.

Unless you tell
them what to
tell you.

You have a favorite film
director. And it isn't
Ronnie Howard.

*

You know which wine
to bring.

*

Sales clerks don't mess
with you.

You've gotten over your
crush on Mel Gibson.

✱

You have a medicine chest
stocked for any occasion.

✱

You have at least one
movie musical on
videotape.

You know the differences between beluga, osetra, and sevruga. And you know which party to bring each to.

•

You make a great Caesar salad. Or at least know where to get one.

You have a favorite
painter. And it's not
LeRoy Neiman.

*

You're not embarrassed to
sing in a piano bar.

*

You're embarrassed
by people who sing in
piano bars.

You never hold a grudge
for longer than a decade
or two.

•

You believe inanimate
objects can actually have
souls. Wigs, for example.

You know how to make a
strategic exit.

•

You don't have a favorite
game show.

You worry about people
you don't even know.
Like Liza Minnelli.

•

Your dog has at least one
holiday outfit.

•

You think big boobs are
hilarious.

You know
at least one
drop-dead
secret about
each of your
siblings.

The only stretch marks
you worry about getting
are on your biceps.

•

You've inhaled.

•

You can be bitchy without
anyone blaming it on
biology.

You have a favorite
I Love Lucy episode.

•

You felt immense personal
gratification when you
heard about Eddie
Murphy and that
drag-queen hooker.

You've just about
defeated the accent you
were born with.

•

You know how to kick
someone out of bed.

•

You know the way
to a man's heart isn't
necessarily through
his stomach.

You choose the most
fabulous greeting cards.

●

You are the last, best hope
of liquor and cigarette
advertisers.

●

You can sniff out big fat
liars in "chat rooms."

You notice physical attributes that others ignore. Thumbs, for instance.

•

You know how to program your VCR.

•

You know every film ever made with male frontal nudity.

You're a friend of a friend
of Bette Midler's.

•

You know which bars to
stay out of.

•

You've got sunscreen
at every conceivable
SPF level.

You have the latest
International Male
catalog.

●

You wouldn't dream of
dressing out of the latest
International Male
catalog.

You wear the appropriate
underwear for each of
your dates.

*

You have a cologne display
worthy of Bloomingdale's.

*

You've stopped using
cologne.

You understand, viscerally,
Joan Crawford.

*

You don't buy generic
brand anything.

*

You don't have a Planet
Hollywood jacket.

Nobody bitches at you for leaving the toilet seat up.

•

You've had at least one boyfriend from a foreign country.

•

You are a special marketing niche. For example, those briefs with the built-in butt falsies.

You have ripped jeans that
don't fit you, hanging in
your closet.

They're your favorite pair.

◆

You have a chest that's
more developed than most
cover girls'.

◆

All your friends know
exactly what'll set your
teeth on edge.

You are responsible for the
revival of the martini.

●

You are not responsible
for the development of the
Fuzzy Navel.

●

Although you're not
responsible for originating
"Sex on the Beach,"
you've had it.

You will
forgive that
great guy who
never called
you back.
Sometime
in the next
millennium.

Some of your best friends
are your ex-lovers.

❋

You have a secret
obsesson with an obscure
cult actress. Say, Julie
Newmar.

You know, definitively,
the sexual predilections
of people you have no
hope of ever meeting.

•

You can make someone
in a hospital bed laugh
out loud.

You know when to play
dumb.

*

You know what to do for
a hangover.

*

You can recite the names
of all of Elizabeth Taylor's
husbands.

Beautiful women trust you.

•

Yes, you do have a
condom.

•

You know which day is
really your anniversary.

You've dated someone
whose name ends in a
vowel.

●

You know the term Divine
refers to:

a. Maria Callas
b. a dead drag queen
c. God
d. all of the above

You have a favorite
Madonna period.

◆

You've called someone
"girlfriend" who is
perhaps neither a girl
nor a friend.

Your favorite spectator
sport is:

1. men's figure skating
2. men's singles tennis
3. men's volleyball
4. men's locker room

One or more of the following apply to you:

a. you adore Judy Garland
b. you hate Judy Garland
c. you hate people who adore Judy Garland
d. you hate people who hate Judy Garland
e. you don't give a damn about Judy Garland
f. who's Judy Garland?

You can supply the last
names to the following list:

 a. Marilyn
 b. Barbra
 c. Andrew Lloyd

＊

You can supply the first
names to the following list:

 a. Garbo
 b. Ciccione
 c. . . . that jerk!

You've dated someone
named Michael.

•

You know that Tennessee
Williams is not a sub-
brand of Jack Daniel's.

•

You know never to play
leapfrog with a unicorn.

You've always
wanted to be a
bicycle seat.

You made Donna Summer
a star.

·

You made Donna Summer
a has-been.

·

You admire people who
stand up to the LAPD.
Like Zsa Zsa.

You don't need a "place at the table." People want to sit at yours.

●

You have your own definition of promiscuous.

●

You have no desire to be President. But, First Lady...well...

If a fat little Polish girl
can grow up to be Martha
Stewart, you can be
anyone you want.

•

Your idea of witty
conversation isn't last
night's Letterman jokes.

Women actually enjoy it
when you're chivalrous.

*

You can have lesbian
tendencies.

*

Tanning salons were
invented for you.

You know
how to make
an entrance.

·

You know
when to make
an exit.

You know when
the party's over.

•

You know where
to go after the
party's over.

Before you had your
current career, you
waited tables.

•

Until your career takes
off, you're waiting tables.

•

Before you were
a bartender, you
waited tables.

•

You're really terrific at
cleaning up after a party.

At the beach, you
dress like a starlet
at Cannes.

•

At the beach,
if you can't dress
like a starlet at
Cannes, you favor
Mother Teresa.

You're fearless about
fighting the elements.
Especially gravity.

●

You know the right words
to say in at least one other
language.

"Working it" at the gym
means:

1. your abs
2. your triceps
3. your deltoids
4. "it"

Your definition of a
"meaningful relationship"
is with:

1. your lover of six years
   or more
2. the lover you just spent
   the weekend with
3. your next lover
4. your tropical fish

Your usual source of
news is:

1. CNN
2. the *New York Times*
3. your car radio
4. your favorite bartender

•

You know about forty-
three synonyms for a
certain male organ.

"Don't ask, don't tell" means:

1. an unworkable military policy
2. you're working on monogamy issues with your lover
3. Oh. Still living with your parents?

•

You can leave this book out on your coffee table.

You can laugh in bed.

•

You can suppress your
laughter in bed.

•

When you hear "a stitch
in time saves nine," you
think of:

1. your grandma
2. your face-lift
3. John Wayne Bobbitt

Three people you don't
want to meet in a dark
alley are:

1. Antonin Scalia
2. Anthony Kennedy
3. Clarence Thomas

◆

Three people you do want
to meet in a dark alley are:

1. Jack Scalia
2. John F. Kennedy, Jr.
3. Long Dong Silver

You can leave the
lights on.

*

You can take a long walk
on a short pier.

*

You can cruise without
being anywhere near
the water.

You know that pigs and bears are not necessarily rural wildlife.

*

You know that kissing a toad rarely turns him into a prince.

You never have to find
her "G" spot.

•

Your roommate can be
your roommate and not
your "roommate."

•

You know that referring
to someone as "a real
lady" isn't necessarily
a compliment.

You actually get a kick out
of having your cigarette
lit by another guy.

*

You find "coming out"
stories fascinating.

*

You are tolerant of
straight sex. Even Jeff
Stryker's.

You never use your age
as an excuse.

*

Your favorite accessory
may also be your dinner
companion.

*

You know that the most
important part of a
party's decor is the
catering staff.

You're most used to
hearing "God, I wish you
were straight" from:

1. your mother
2. your best straight
   female friend
3. your lover

You can match these
objects of fetish with their
proper locations:

a. handcuffs
b. rubber
c. sling
d. jockstrap
e. whatever

1. gym
2. dungeon
3. body of water
4. four-poster bed
5. whatever

If your cat's a female, you
swear it's a lesbian.

•

If your cat's a male, you
swear it's a lesbian.

•

You've sung in the shower.
Or at least hit some
high notes.

Unlike most straight guys,
you've practiced your
Kegel exercises. (Even if
you never knew it.)

•

You've bought at least
one novelty item for a
woman friend who was
too embarrassed to do
it for herself.

You're often the "best man" at weddings. And you're often the best man at weddings, too.

◆

You sing along heartily with songs that make most feminists cringe, like "Stand by Your Man."

You've been to a bris.
You've been to a christen-
ing. You've been to a "new
age" service. You've been
to a first communion.
You've been to a seance.

You have a carefully
considered evaluation of
the food after each.

You feel comfortable moisturizing. You feel natural having a facial. You've investigated liposuction. You've researched Rogaine. You've become knowledgeable about every form of hair replacement.

You feel just fine about getting older.

You enjoy flirting.

*

You enjoy teasing.
And not just wigs.

*

Unlike most mammals,
your courtship rituals
often begin after mating
has taken place.

You are amused
by the presump-
tion of straight
guys who assume
you want them.

·

You are amused
by straight guys
who want you.

You can have a passionate
relationship without it
necessarily being physical.

•

You can have a physical
relationship without
it necessarily being
passionate.

When straight women say you're "not on our bus," you don't correct them. Even though you wouldn't be caught dead on a bus.

•

Your pets send greeting cards.

When someone tells you
he's a runway model, you
restrain yourself from
saying, "Which airport?"

*

You don't think it's sappy
to hold hands at the
movies.

You have a carefully se-
lected Yiddish vocabulary.

*

You don't ever have to be
"more like your brother."

*

At least one torch song
really hits home for you.

You know that being a
closet queen explains
every kind of antisocial
behavior.

•

You've never felt the urge
to drink too much beer,
jump in your Camaro with
your buddies, and go out
straight-bashing.

Your favorite "action"
movies have nothing to do
with Sylvester Stallone.

•

You'll never have to hear
your mother complain
about your wife.

•

Your idea of a "great
evening at the theater"
is not spending it with
Jackie Mason.

You have at least one cocktail specialty.

⁂

You never have to plan your vacations around the school year.

⁂

A two-seater convertible seems perfectly practical to you.

You never have to worry about getting lipstick on your collar. Unless, of course, it's your own.

You always have a chilled
bottle in your fridge.

●

You know where to get
impressive party nibbles.

●

For you, proselytizing is
not a duty. But it can be
a pleasure.

You're conversant with
every fashion trend. With
the possible exception of
Lesbian Chic.

❖

You have a favorite
character from a Disney
animated feature. And it's
one of the nasty ones.

You have at least one frat
brother who's also a sister.

•

You've dated several men
whose first names are
last names.

•

You have at least one CD
in a language other than
English.

You know what the following have in common:

1. Roddy McDowell
2. Liam Neeson
3. James Woods
4. Ewan McGregor

(Hint: It's *not* that they're actors.)

There's at least one category of music that you cannot abide.

•

You didn't "choose" to be gay. It was sheer luck.

•

You've never been moshed.

You've "gone all the
way" with a woman. But
fortunately you found
your way back.

•

You don't have an
"alternative lifestyle."
An "alternative lifestyle"
would be heterosexuality.

Cats like you.

◆

During your life, you have:

1. embraced your feminine side
2. embraced your masculine side
3. embraced someone else's masculine side

You've been tempted by
the Seven Deadly Sins.
And you have a favorite.

•

Everyone's still waiting for
your "comeuppance."

•

Your idea of exhilarating
entertainment is not sitting
in front of an enormous TV.
(Unless it's RuPaul.)

You've left someone totally
speechless.

You know never to disturb
an artist. Especially if he's
cutting your hair.

Your parents did not make
you a homosexual. So you
had to go out and make
one yourself.

•

You're acutely aware
of personal hygiene.

•

You only need to be
married to your career.

You're truly
a Good
Samaritan.
You're always
ready to give
another guy
a hand.

You feel one of two ways about opera:

1. you can name every Puccini heroine and the diva most closely associated with the role
2. the only one you'll sit through has Susan Lucci in it

Your idea of the perfect man is:

1. Cary Grant
2. Sean Connery
3. Harrison Ford
4. Keanu Reeves
5. Grace Jones

You know not to go
to weddings to find a
potential mate.

•

You've shaved something
other than your face.

The smell of leather brings
to mind:

a. a brand new car
b. your favorite jacket
c. last night's date

*

You always know the
best place in town to get
anything.

When you hear "Surrey with the Fringe on Top," you think:

1. it's a grand night for singing
2. get me outta here
3. Hair Club for Men

You get to pick the
restaurant.

*

It is not assumed that
you'll pick up the check.

You know that Stonewall
is:

1. a Civil War general
2. a delaying tactic
3. Connecticut for fence
4. a great excuse to put on
   some drag every year
   and kick up your heels

You know when to stay
in bed.

❋

You've got some terrific
dirty jokes.

❋

You can read between the
lines in a "personals" ad.

You keep your nose
hairs clipped.

*

Even if you're in Kansas,
you're not in Kansas
anymore.

You can see past the
vulgarity of construction
workers.

•

You've got your own
section at the local video
store. (As long as it's not
Blockbuster.)

•

You can lip-synch to at
least one Supremes song.

You know how
to dish.

You know how
to diss.

You know how
to dust.

You don't have to wait
till Halloween to wear
something frightening.

●

You don't have to have
a favorite *Seinfeld*
character.

Your idea of a "girl group" is:

1. the Supremes
2. the Spice Girls
3. Saturday night in Chelsea

A walk on the beach can
reap benefits beyond
burning calories.

*

You don't assume that
women at the party will
do the cleaning up.

*

You've made sunbathing
a performance art.

You don't wear fur.

*

When faced with great
physical pain, you do not
hesitate. Like having your
back waxed.

All your friends do not
have to "get along."

•

You have your own
definition of "decadent."
It probably refers
to a dessert.

You have a large collection of anniversary pictures. They may be with different guys, however.

You can be truly objective
when your married friends
have spats.

•

We've got Gore Vidal.
They've got Al Gore.

When you say you "did a number," it means you:

1. sang like Ethel Merman
2. behaved like Ethel Merman
3. slept with someone who looks like Ernest Borgnine

You're essentially
an optimist. It's
why you always
have a spare
toothbrush.

If you're
feeling especially
optimistic, you
take it with you
to the bars.

You'd make a very
conscientious father.

❖

You've made a very
conscientious father.

❖

You're not easily
impressed.

❖

If there are gay bars in
Lapland, you'll find 'em.

You're the "peacemaker"
in the family.

⬥

You're an extremely
generous host.

⬥

Your glassware doesn't
have Ronald McDonald
on it.

You're well acquainted
with the following
locations:

1. The Village
2. West Hollywood
3. South Beach
4. Oz

The only card tricks you
do are in your address
book.

●

You know which flowers
to bring.

●

You know how and when
to apologize.

You've made Halloween
an important national
holiday.

♦

You can make the sourest
nurse laugh.

♦

Your "love handles" are
sometimes actually used
as such.

You have a
favorite piece of
classical music.
Even if it's
"These Boots
Are Made for
Walking."

You've always got the most
interesting coffee-table
books.

•

When someone turns his
back on you, you consider
it an opportunity.

•

You've got a large
assortment of movie-star
biographies.

You have your own
restaurants.

●

You have your own discos.

●

You have your own
bookstores.

●

You have your own
coffee bars.

You have your own
movie theaters.

●

You have your own
travel agents.

●

You have your own
financial advisers.

●

You have your own money.

When *GQ* started ignoring
you, they went straight
downhill.

•

You can spot a cheap suit.
Even if it's in a heap on
your bedroom floor.

•

You can work the
Classifieds sections for
fun or profit.

You only lose expensive sunglasses.

You can always "whip up a little something." You may even have a little whip.

You're not breathlessly awaiting the *Sports Illustrated* swimsuit issue.

●

You admire Cindy Crawford for her marketing acumen.

●

If you were Claudia Schiffer, you wouldn't be with David Copperfield.

You know where to find
a meat rack. And it ain't
in your kitchen drawer.

•

You have a romantic
side. It can be face-up
or face-down.

You forgive,
but you never
forget.

•

You forget,
but you never
forgive.

You know how to get out
the really tough stains.

•

There's always someone
who'll help you move out.
Even if it's your present
cohabitant.

•

You can't be fooled, but
you can be had.

There are several different
ways in which you can lose
your virginity.

*

You'll probably never
have to explain the facts
of life to a child.

*

You don't get into fistfights
at Little League games.

You have a certain *je ne sais quoi.* You're known for your *joie de vivre.*

You know at least two French phrases.

Your role models can be
of either sex.

•

It's unlikely anyone will
ask you, "So, when are
you two going to start a
family?"

•

You have a sexual
persuasion with its
own flag.

You've been on the right
side of a boycott.

•

You can survive a messy
breakup.

•

You understand the sub-
text in "buddy" movies.

•

You're still "going through
a phase." It's called
adulthood.

The boyfriends of your women friends are jealous of you for the right reasons.

*

You don't mind sharing your toys.

*

You have a favorite jazz singer.

You don't go to comedy
clubs to see straight male
stand-up comedians.

•

You don't buy books
written by straight male
stand-up comedians.

•

You don't go to movies
starring straight male
stand-up comedians.

You always root for some-
one in the midst of a come-
back. Except, perhaps,
Andrew "Dice" Clay.

•

You are more likely to
quote Silverstone than
Schwarzenegger.

•

It's unlikely you'll ever
be forced into a "shotgun
wedding."

Your idea of a festive
night out is not the local
Bennigan's.

•

You have a favorite Rob
Lowe performance (ahem)
on video.

•

You see the attempt to
demolish the NEA as a
personal affront.

You know the
relative merits
of every kind of
underwear.

You know
the relative
merits of no
underwear.

You know exactly how
many martinis it takes.

●

You know when a fashion
trend is over.

●

At some moment in your
life, you've envisioned
having backup girls.

Your favorite picture is:

1. Andy Warhol's
   Marilyn Monroe
2. George Cukor's
   A Star Is Born
3. Brad Pitt's on the
   Internet

*

You have a cherished list
of hilariously bad movies.

You've been through "looking for love in all the wrong places." And sometimes the wrong places are all right.

•

You suspect a passion for Tibet or Scientology indicates something repressed.

Your definition of
"swing" is:

a. what Ella Fitzgerald
   does
b. what a lesbian does
   during Dinah Shore
   Weekend
c. what you fervently hope
   Harrison Ford does

Your straight girlfriends
can use you as a reality
check.

*

You know your enemies.

*

You can do hypocrisy
checks on Liz Smith.

You know how you'd
spend David Geffen's
money.

•

We've got James Dean.
They've got Jimmy Dean.

•

You know lust is no
substitute for love. But
it sure beats knitting.

After a
workout at
the gym,
you feel like
a new man.
Fortunately,
he's right there
in the shower.

Your idea of a hot boutique
is not the Dockers Shop.

•

You don't select a
restaurant based upon
all-you-can-eat specials.

•

Contrary to popular
belief, you know how to
handle a screwdriver.
(Even one without vodka.)

164

You have absolutely no delusions about sailors.

•

If you're only 2 percent of the population, who were all those other guys marching in Washington in '93?

A list of girl things you can
use if you care to:

1. fishnets
2. eyelash curlers
3. bidets
4. *Playgirl*
5. somebody else's
   husband

A list of gender-neutral things you can use if you care to:

1. cucumbers
2. sleep masks
3. Absolut
4. *The New Yorker*
5. k. d. lang CDs

You have mixed feelings
about the fact that being
"gay for pay" now includes
the likes of Tom Hanks,
Kevin Kline, and Patrick
Swayze.

✳

Even if you've never had
one before, you now have
a favorite sportscaster:
Marv Albert.

You've raised eyebrows.

•

You've raised more than eyebrows.

You know that a slap is not
necessarily an invitation
to fight.

●

Your mom probably never
caught you with a stack of
Playboys under the bed.

●

If you were a Boy Scout,
you were always prepared.

The "love that dares not
speak its name" is now
blabbing every other day
on *Oprah*.

◆

You're a believer in
Modern design. With the
possible exception of that
"less is more" stuff.

You're Barbra Streisand's biggest fan.

•

You know that Barbra Streisand's biggest fan is Barbra Streisand.

•

You know precisely at which point Michael Jackson should have stopped with the surgery, already.

Sometimes you're Lucy. Sometimes you're Ethel. Sometimes you can even be Ricky. But you're never, ever, Fred.

You're first with the
really juicy rumors. Like
Travolta/Stallone, for
example.

•

You're far more flexible
than most men your age.

You don't like the term
"open homosexual."
It makes you sound like
a 7-Eleven.

•

Not only have you added
spice to your sex life—
sometimes you've added
side dishes.

Hopefully, you
don't slur other
minorities.

•

Hopefully, if you
do slur other
minorities,
someone shuts
you up.

You don't look to your
parents for political
guidance.

•

You have a sentimental
collection of objects that
are of no interest to anyone else. Pez dispensers,
for example.

You can immediately
audit the flaws of
anyone your friends
are considering going
home with.

●

You know when *not* to
listen to your friends.

You've overheard bar
conversations like these:

Man 1: You hurt my
　　　　　feelings!
Man 2: Both of them?

or

Man 1: He says he's
　　　　　bisexual.
Man 2: It's true. He has
　　　　　to buy sex.

You're generally aware
of your "issues."

•

You know that one of
the highest compliments
you can give a woman is
to comment on her
weight loss.

You know never to
respond to the question,
"How old do you think
I am?"

•

You can actually have
slept with someone before
your first "date."

You believe in nondiscrimination. But you struggle with the challenge of cute straight guys working in gay clubs.

●

You know that accepting a cocktail from a stranger is tantamount to announcing your engagement.

You've kept certain
tattered cocktail napkins
and matchbook covers for
sentimental reasons.

●

You know that when
someone is described
as a "man's man,"
he often is.

You enjoy women who call other women "broads."

•

You do not enjoy straight men who call women "gals."

You know the only accepta-
ble use of "girls" refers to
prepubescent women or
post-pubescent men.

◆

You know that, aside
from the Westminster
Kennel Club, the term
"bitch" has no gender
whatsoever.

You may have enjoyed the '70s, but you don't miss the nylon shirts, bell bottoms, and platform shoes.

•

The only thing that interests you about the '70s are the nylon shirts, bell bottoms, and platform shoes.

You know Marky
Mark lost his
appeal the instant
he opened his
mouth.

•

You know Marky
Mark can regain his
appeal the instant
he opens his mouth.

You know that "small talk" can be about spirituality or politics, and "important issues" can be about hair.

◆

You've actually lived out some of your fantasies.

You have your own
definition of the term
"faithful."

●

You've outgrown your
interest in David Bowie.

●

Your male bonding rituals
have nothing to do with
beating drums or running
wild through the woods.

You never took Ronald
Reagan seriously.

•

You always took Nancy
Reagan seriously.

•

You know that Jane
Wyman never took either
one of them seriously.

You know that everyone has a certain something that distinguishes him or her. And you're especially curious about Michael Jackson and Bill Clinton.

The only religious cult you've ever considered joining was that of Madonna, Mother of Lourdes.

•

You have no interest in Mormon doctrine. But polygamy might be worth a shot.

You know a supermarket
checkout when you see
one. And yes, you deliver.

*

You'd never consider
stabbing someone in the
back. It's much more fun
seeing his face.

Perhaps someone has
called you "catty."
Probably a dog.

•

You've been cruised by
someone who looked just
like a classic movie star.
(Charles Laughton)

Unlike most
straight women,
you have no
problem being
treated solely
as a sexual
object.

You're resentful about
sexual inequality. After
all, you've done everything
Pamela Harriman did,
and *you* didn't get to be
Ambassador to France.

❖

You know that paying
"lip service" is not always
a negative thing.

You know that some of
the worst social functions
can be redeemed by two
magical words: Open Bar.

·

That men are from Mars
and women are from
Venus is irrelevant. You're
far more concerned with
Uranus.

You know that:

1. getting aroused during a physical examination by a male doctor does not make you a homosexual

2. having occasional same-sex fantasies does not make you a homosexual

3. having impotence problems with women does not make you a homosexual

4. getting drunk and "accidentally" having sex with one of your best buddies does not make you a homosexual

5. straight guys have a vast ability to rationalize what things do not make them homosexual

If you're a true
Manhattanite, you
wouldn't be caught dead
in Queens. At least not
the borough.

❋

You know guys who call
themselves "tops." But
you can get 'em to spin.

We've got Barneys.
They've got Barney.

•

You know your body is a
temple. It's just that you
welcome all denominations.

A list of guy things you'll
never have to deal with:

1. Aqua Velva
2. brown socks
3. a vasectomy
4. powdered rhino horn
5. a female virgin

A list of girl things you'll
never have to deal with:

1. IUDs
2. estrogen replacement
3. the Lifetime Channel
4. strawberry douche
5. lip bleach

You have no doubts about the accuracy of the Kinsey Report.

•

Happily, men are not self-conscious about taking their tops off in public.

•

Your individuality is not asserted solely by your choice of tie.

You don't assume every
woman in power has slept
her way to the top and/or
is a lesbian.

·

You have some interesting
marketing ideas. But
you're still waiting for the
FTD "Pride Bouquet."

"Is That All There Is?"

brings to mind:

1. a Peggy Lee song
2. lunch at the
   Canyon Ranch
3. the gay scene in Tulsa
4. a date who's evidently
   been abusing steroids

You know how to open
champagne.

•

You can buy someone
a gift that makes them
scream.

You know, by heart, every line in:

1. your high-school musical
2. *All About Eve*
3. *The Rocky Horror Picture Show*
4. your face

You know how to write a
thank-you note.

*

You get as much mileage
out of a ripped T-shirt as
Stanley Kowalski.

*

You can tell whether you'll
relate to someone by their
hairdo.

You're the one who gets
to demolish pompous
straight men.

●

You helped defeat
Bob Dornan.

●

You know which clothes
to throw out.

You can name at least
four matinee idols from
the '50s who share your
proclivities.

•

Your perfect vacation
does not involve short
people wearing big plastic
Disney heads.

You have something silk in
your wardrobe that isn't
worn around the neck.

•

You can wear any color
you want.

You know how to cook at
least one seduction dinner.

◆

You look natural wearing
an earring. Even a clip-on.

You don't have to like
everybody.

✴

You always keep your nails
very neatly trimmed.

You can match the follow-
ing wardrobe articles:

1. cut-offs
2. ascot
3. press-on nails
4. bandanna

a. golden retriever
b. work boots
c. martini, straight-up
d. "Cher" wig

You know in which city,
and on what dates, the
exact same Circuit Party
revolves, all year long.

*

You look like a Ralph
Lauren model.

*

You look like a Ralph
Lauren display.

People tell you that you resemble: River Phoenix, Andy Garcia, Denzel Washington, or Sean Connery. People *don't* tell you that you resemble: Beavis, Cheech Marin, Sherman Helmsley, or Marie Dressler.

You know how to make
your boss look good.

●

You know how to make
your boss look bad.

●

You know when to get a
new job.

You know your flaws.

●

You know how to conceal
your flaws.

●

You are *always* ready for
your close-up.

●

Your favorite steps are:

1. the Bunny Hop
2. the Hustle
3. the Two-Step
4. the Twelve-Step

219

You have 412 ways to
tell someone to get lost.
Approximately 136 are
nonverbal.

●

You never have to respond
to the question, "How
'bout those Mets?"

●

You know that Quentin
Crisp is not a cereal by
Quaker Oats.

You're known for your
taste. And if you're not,
nobody dares tell you.

*

You get along better with
your boyfriend's mother
than he does.

*

You can dance.

You've got a large
collection of amusing
baseball caps.

◆

You are difficult to shock.

◆

Your friends say you're
a nasty person with a
nice streak.

You've dated someone who looks just like one of the Baldwins. (Of course, that includes the pianos.)

You define "beach ball" as:

1. a multicolored, blow-up plastic object
2. the Morning Party
3. what happens with a cute guy at the Morning Party

You can tolerate the feature
articles about straight sex
in *Men's Health*.

•

You actually enjoy the
ballet. Well, at least
the outfits.

•

You believe every rumor
you don't start yourself.

You've set your VCR
for every conceivable
entertainment awards
show.

⬦

You can have an incestuous
relationship with your
"father figure."

You've
spent many a
sleepless night.
They're your
favorites.

You can walk right past
someone and still let them
know you're interested.

*

You've never been accused
of being a prude.

*

You always have cab fare.

Your favorite master of the
Italian Renaissance is:

a. Michelangelo
b. Caravaggio
c. da Vinci
d. Armani

When throwing a party,
you know how to put out
quite a spread. Sometimes
after the party, too.

*

Your idea of a happy meal
doesn't include Chicken
McNuggets.

*

Brunch was invented
for you.

Your favorite artificially sweetened concoction is:

1. Diet Peach Snapple
2. rum and Diet Coke with a squeeze of lime
3. Kathie Lee Gifford

You resent any
assumptions
made about you
because of your
sexuality—
including about
half the ones
in this book.